IN A FREE STATE

ALSO BY P.R. ANDERSON

Litany Bird
(Carapace Poets, 2000)

Foundling's Island
(UCT Writer's Series, 2007;
REPUBLISHED BY UHLANGA, 2018)

IN A FREE STATE

A MUSIC

BY

P. R. ANDERSON

UHLANGA

2018

In a Free State

© P. R. Anderson, 2018, all rights reserved

Published in Cape Town, South Africa by uHlanga in 2018

UHLANGAPRESS.CO.ZA

Distributed outside South Africa by the African Books Collective

AFRICANBOOKSCOLLECTIVE.COM

ISBN: 978-0-620-81224-5

Edited by Francine Simon

Cover design and typesetting by Nick Mulgrew

The body text of this book is set in Garamond Premier Pro 11PT on 15PT

In memoriam

A.R.B.

"Nokomfu"

Come April and the cosmos
resumes the ditches, flushing
seeps that were hidden or hid
their transient crake, where frogs woke,
—so now there's paint spilled, lying
on the broken ground, whitewash,
rose-wash, eyewash, lovely, cold
as the coming days. It's time
to cover, and crossing fields
or waiting in seemingly
pointless places, on gravel
or under zinc, people have
put on blankets already
and turn their faces to shine
their covered eyes at the sun.
The soot of diesel sweetens
local winds, the kinds that chase
buses or rubbish, or butt
down the sugar-hoarded leaves
divorcing their poplars, writs
that began as love-letters
in a summer fling. Old flames
now, they kindle winter fires
in the cuttings, or compost
unwilling ground, the annual
drought, whose one water is frost,
whose blue skies creak with crows.

1

1

Nor police nor hare-finder find
her burnt owl on the *qhobosheane*, Merabeng hill.
It canters in the poor light of events,

2

a dead shrub in the wind. Now you
have the prototype angel, moving on
one singed, saluting wing, body of sodden

3

shuttlecock. But the enormous spurs
bounce on the back of the world,
and the eyes, the eyes have it.

2

1

A language of vowels, sleeptalk.
The wrack of consonants is washed away.
Plains speech, ridged palates, porridge

2

cooking day-long in a black drum on
coal and rubbish. Concord.
The drill of the phrase put, puttering

3

two-stroke. A tongue like song. To your
tin ear it should be called "Among". Falling fine-
sounding into the cradle of smallest bones.

3

1

For want of a story we will lie, lie
at the ramparts of our teeth's Jericho.
How imperfectly we know

2

this girl and how we fill her in.
Built of winter sun and grief, embodied,
she is not beyond our ken, found

3

wanting, swerving into the aftermath
called self, a new life in the cluttered
redoubt of rocks, or words, or sin.

4

1

And in the *Courant*s and *Advertiser*s,
in their one type, on pages
fined with meal, wrestle a taxonomy:

2

war of the wire and beacons, also the war of the left-hand cairns;
stock-war; war of the handshake, also the comrades; war of water,
also the war of the Gariep; war of the generations; war of the clans
of cat and not-cat; war of the kinds of grain; trot-combat; church
war, also war of the *weiboere*; war of the blockhouse, also of the
roadblock; war of the railway;

3

war of the ford of Jabbok; war of the famine-thong; war of the
black peaches; war of the watchtower mortared with bitumen;
war of the balloons, Bloedfontein; war of the Asking; war of the
common enemy; war over the uncollateral sea; war of the Anthill,
also of incomers and runaways; Rebellion; war of the Treaty, also the
Concession; war of the mud river, the dry river, the sand river and
the great river.

5

1

And the thin parliament: *Pitso ea Dinoneana*,
Meeting of the Birds. And such. And then
they bought maize from Australia.

2

Kromdraai: the graveyard and rusting vehicles
skittled, like carcasses of the rinderpest.
To work, laying rail, more or less everywhere.

3

Do not preach me that sermon supposed.
I was alive and in that way, and there joined you
smashed dead. September, thirty years ago.

6

1
Smoke and wind as we are, yet
we are given days to reckon scab
millet, red corn, complain of our bones. So
2
what is our life but a bone
in the body? What is smoke but the bone
of the wind? Millet
3
for counting the days, days for counting
the millet. So what is a body but
counting bones in the smoke?

7

1

What provokes the frost is the mourning clothes:
sun lies with the bitter grass as sheep's gall in water.
She is gripped.

2

She is standing in the winter sun in a trap
of brick wall out of sight
of the world, thin wind

3

spun in the Malutis and her eyes
are half-way coddled by the morning light.
Winter sun and her back to the brick.

8

1

Vilified in black reckoning on a white account,
always another version. Even after
all they record only her beauty.

2

MaNthatisi, Mosayane, none but adore
her like men making her up. Nor should
the byword 'Little Woman' be

3

thought other than the fierce
iron in irony, a fugitive
defiance. Dust, ashes, mayhem by night.

9

1

Mornings I take my own death
as it comes. Yours, should I
get it entire in mind, shreds

2

the contract. I have only the conclave
of your final instants to go on,
night watch of the slow

3

split second. Lethal clutter of physics.
Can you scream as a question?
And the knot of lights.

10

1

Am I spoiled in the yard? She is arrayed
before him dressed in nard,
paraffin, carbolic, acetone, thus

2

swathed in the censed hour under iron.
Corpse: a church sweet in every pore.
His eyes break to her like oil in the morning sun.

3

She will not pay the shilling passage in a free state,
but wets her hand on his face; history comes
free to the keen, and to the unwilling free.

11

1

Never again put your hand to
the warm brick. Winter sun was the first
gold won under heaven.

2

Touch it and you trust it.
False. Into that honey sinks
angel or fly in equal amber.

3

At the edge of Welkom you go round
the circles in such dopey light
forever, they are so wide, so *circular*.

12

1

Now he is standing before her with
cooking oil in his eyes. She is seeing
him with his own eyes too much.

2

Where is my blanket? I am cold.

I am called at the cars, you can hear the calling.
I will try to find the way back to you in the months.

3

It is like geese in the morning.
The iron cracks like shooting in the morning.
His eyes are breaking like oil.

13

1
Edinu. Plain, steppe.
We have it from Sumer.
We are icumen in. But let me

2
remind you of your *Paradise Lost*,
crossing the Gariep in one bound,
as Nimrod, son of Cush,

3
builder of Babel. Welcome
to this our *fair equality,*
fraternal state.

Earth is issuing to us out
of a congress of mountains
an angel's wing strewn with agate.
Ponies travail in the ice
levels, *hup! hup!*, and goats knock
their bells. An orange jet prays
in the gutter of itself,
asking its way forward, what
is this soughing? And then there
is no end of it again.

14

1
Conditions of Orange. For how
long will things be? You have not seen

2
the light until
a warbler belts it out: a gape

3
of flame, mouth of the marrow flower.
Prince of Orange.

15

1

Now on this random upland girt
by pink-footed falcons out of Amur,
construe rubbles and sediments, stow

2

violence a day away in fundamental coal,
drag fetched-up seas, assay impact
silicates, igneous tripes, excavate

3

spider-tumours of crystal, delve rare
metals, basalt hackles, the weak wax
Babylons of sandstone priested by ibis.

16

1
She is on tiptoe, twelve, who reaches back
into the child she was before the wall,

2
a finger into herself and signs
the back of his hand

3
with herself and says
I am going to die.

We are nowhere in a free
state, but avid as lithium.
Never was an age of gold
but trouble. As iron sings
in the shadow of the valley,
shod hoof to cobble anvil
and in the stage-thunder
of alloys shaken in the wings,
we forge and bang our bell and
ask *What are we calling for?*
A sign? *But signs are hapless.*
Happens is what signifies.

17

1

Seams of residual grass burn as lava,
gradual as coal, coal of winter nights.
Flightless lightning, brittle vessels of grass.

2

Seething at dawn, ash
and sublimate of frost among the soft,
remaindered flames, the tenebrous

3

at the choke. Charcoal, perished plastics,
glass unmade, cans buckled by their own
jaundiced golds, mornings after.

18

1

Priest with his vestments
over one arm locking the vestry, cigarette
in hand, the body now

2

stowed in a black Chevrolet, in a dwindling dust.
A girl cannot reckon the tenses, running
into the world rendered, or pull the gall

3

from the water, sweat of her eyes. Across
those rivers she lights out for the Free State.
I have gathered the gall, believe me.

19

1

——from David's Grave,
at the confluence of the Riet and Modder Rivers; thence
along the Riet River to where Krom Elbow Spruit falls

2

into the said Riet River; thence Krom Elbow Spruit
to the land occupied by the chief Le Pui,
thence along the said Orange River as far as Ramah;

3

and thence in a direct line to David's Grave aforesaid.
All title is theft; the earth refuses all, whom
it will take down. You and I: the aforesaid.

Sky stoops to ridge and ridge
spreads its plover's wing, raises
the hackles of an angel.
Aloes put up their ferrous
staves to the sunward and root
down in an agate gravel;
our geological angel
is argussed with wicks of flame.
Who believe that they speak, are
silent, or do anything
else from a free decree of mind,
dream with their eyes open.

20

1

Voyage d'Exploration aux Montagnes Bleues.
Where else take your prot heart, but into the least
churched souls, seated cross-legged

2

under God? And the mountains *are* a blue
rubble; play station of the Lord.
Thermals bear prayer aloft, aloft,

3

unbarbered vultures sail for saints. Look
in, there is your refuge and your blue
massif central.

21

1

Damn me if she doesn't leave it all
unsaid! She got free of the dolorous, finite,
prosy ache. There's no end to it.

2

More of the same. More sad boys out
of orbit and their depth, more homeward
bounding, more bodies in a hearse

3

on a rusted axle. —She? Damn her.
She is your unfinished symphony. I beg
you, let her be.

22

1

Dawn in the colours of a national anthem.
The Ds of dams struck with fire, washing
on the tangential fences, and cormorants.

2

Telephone poles stride west, kestrels
on the wires, turret-down
into the wind out of nowhere

3

going nowhere. The ground
covered: packed ash of *materia*,
unsublimable.

23

1
come the clouds.

2
From the south-west
in a smudge of small war.
From the east without rain,
the scarce cattle of a flight.
Out of nowhere
pile into mountains,

tip ice like locusts,
calve,

3
build silos in eyes.

24

1

Walking on verges, crossing the patchwater, cloud
underfoot, sidestepping the *nooienshaar* of cassette tape's
tangled lightning, evading the burning bush
shod or unshod, they lift their hems to blot a face

2

or to hide it from the God they call down to spurn
for going by on the other side,
and they tidy the thread in their hems and number
the worse-than-war on the skirts of war, crying like jackals

3

over the *appelkoossiekte*, the hotness of being gravid,
the bad breath of rancour, blood running
through the gut of a field of folk, peach trees
fired and shattered, feathers and ash blowing,

and might as well count the ways a child might disappear
as how many have.

25

1

Man rides a bicycle to a farther farm;
wind comes up out of the ditches, plucks
his sleeves. He rides the skeleton

2

of a better idea. Women tie
on their heads the scarves of nations.
The shrub

3

shudders off its myrrh.
On this world, this dibbled lens, this disc,
etc.

26

1

There is no language able of that absence
when knowing must go into the vast
where speech cannot carry. But go, knowing

2

no language to compass the bulked
ceaseless enormity, altars of clouds
without Guest, endlessly consecrating

3

blue to its use. Until a heart must fall
down in its being, baulked, before
a prophecy: of glare, the fact of earth.

27

1
Sun falls in through a blue
window in a welder's daylight.

2
Women are singing, some
in dark glasses, some with far eyes,
joining private sadness to sad song.

3
Lilting east
with tissues in their sleeves.

28

1

All their days are travelling through
them as is the borrowed God
given and dissolved.

2

They are towards a country of shadow.
A country of mountains, a country of shadow.

3

They are trying to bury a heart
in a scraped grave,
but the ground is always melting

29

1
under the wicks of winter poplars
and dwindling west in the long amen
2
of the engine. The women
carry the tune
of dolour into the hills with them.
3
This is the last we shall see
of them. Under that steady sun

30

1
blazoned in a blue window,
2
spoken aloud as one unending
3
gasp, all pass.

31

1

Yet there is pluck to the equipped virgin
miner pictured here: cockaded,
pot-and-coated, bundled of

2

bird-fetching sticks, pipe-smoking, gun-slung.
Guns for diamonds, yes, we have
begotten a human race.

3

The diamonds are passed
back into senselessness. Conjugate: finance, fiancée...
It is their brilliant emptiness.

32

1

On cold trains, in disembarked
clots at taxi halts, people become.
Easy to see the wing of war

2

beat shadow over all, but travel
poses the polity of the living dead, how all
pass through with gut-ache and full bladder

3

and the ail of cares. Money
moves at every station, counted
votives issued as barren shares.

33

1

A cement bag blows in the blue
trailing its grit of bone, dust dun as human
ash, trilling in the pipes of its millefeuille

2

cladding, cardboard smacking itself for cold.
The whole sky's its stadium. On the road
trucks shiver in their tarps, throatsore,

3

and in municipal rockeries Christ Thorn
swarms the dark stone. Out there air
's quick as a roughed gull on a reservoir wall.

34

1

Vowels and history and the dead
weight of the negligible story (her
organised bones bewildering her,

2

who loses speech, becoming said)
drive her to ground.
You burrow her to your purpose

3

in iron mud, shot gravel, so she
can bide geology,
world, weather.

35

1

Baptised Nehemiah, turned out
like Coleridge as an author in the new
and terrible sense of print. History

2

is given 'A Little Light from Basutoland'
(1880). Sekhonyana eludes us perhaps
as an essay must. This much

3

is true: that history is all essay,
coruscating, deathly, wrong.
But what would we not do to fascinate?

36

1

Summer. You say so.
You drag her out with the ants
under a harvest sky reaped

2

with the knives of swifts.
Feed her locusts falling
from a weather of kestrels.

3

Somewhere after the reaved
sheep passing under the smoke
of their trampling, smoke

37

1
of a grassfire, the lovely
whistles of thieves,
somehow after a winter

2
lost in sleep, somewhere
beyond clouds accruing
like treaties, the railway, the far

3
shadows driven like sheep,
you put her there, imperilled
by your putting, and see:

she stays, is stayed.
                                    World
fled into the steady east.

38

1

The Hackles, the Shiners, the Cosmonaut, the Millet,

2

the Eight Days Harvest, the Droves, the Re-wrought Tin, the Ultracity,

3

the Sputnik, the Concertina, the Sheep Knife, the 9-Volt Battery.

39

1

(O but they are gone into stars, all.

O but they are so cold for fires, stars.)

They must be the forebegone,

2

time and distance being alike to them.

Diamond dust, the little boys, milk of the scalding

skillet, milk broken in milk-grass, milk

3

let down, sperm of a flea, skypox,

breath of the cattle, cat's hackles, cloud of statistics.

They are our guess of light.

40

1

I send you a collar worked pretty,
words and flowers hereabouts, in yet
wet-like thread of cotton brighter

2

than a journey morning.
It is a little Christmas.
It is a composite memento:

3

Van Velck's Vley,
Colesberg, Fauresmith. Perhaps
it will last, and who knows who.

41

1

Squashbox keening in a conclave of blankets. Clap
till the words warm, on Thaba Bosiu and round Manyatseng.
So life, a skirling and a yelping, a sobbing and a grasping,

2

the music stays. Fug of paraffin. The music
drills and rattles a mile down into the heat of the stone,
climbs up again to the bunks of the dead,

3

and when cousins go out into the night, hearts
of scald-porridge, it is said in the seed of stars
breathed that when you do you die into a song.

42

1

I had thought alliance was the good itself,
somewhere to sit out the thunder, reason
enough to slaughter, live as if

2

this was the life. All our tomorrows were
in your hands. And every day after came
more of the fire-impelled, the wailing,

3

wanting. I came to you even though I am
metonymically the stronger and I said we can
only do this together, as the thunder said.

43

1

And this is where you almost always are,
speechless with an awe you mistake
for boredom, floating the idea of you

2

as the soul you have to be in order
to survive the tenuous, imperilled fact
you are: sad primate, caught in the violet

3

shunt of auto-glass, lifting your eyes
to the welder's star, itself informing
the sun of its tiredness. Can there be so?

44

1
So brown a light, a reaped
light? See with eyes of maize
and watch till likeness

2
fails your eyes: it seems
a rasp of light drawn
across, a tractor towing

3
its flue of topsoil, a bromine
bled into blue yonder. And maize
rattles like a pan of cheap tea.

45

1
Pass dams delivered of the total
milkshakes of transits, truckers' coffees,
where stints crawl, and bass and barbel
2
sway and grow bland, and
pass ditches where
jackals whelp between
3
rains, and weeds got
of the dung of war
put out their medals.

46

1
Annuities of the kept seed, kept
dry of fire. Diamond burns.
So the first coal we knew, bright vacant

2
nights, interred.
Coal's fire interred.
Seed burns a year down, and

3
I and I only work for you. I come
a cropper on proportion, ploughing
on shares on rugged ground.

What knife of mind cuts the knife-
edge where the ridge runs either
into blue or back into
itself? Always into you.
You hear the ridge hiss as day
does day-long, for its stone clutch
laid on stone, protesting hope
of its radical, skyless
self: stone, stone *ex nihilo*,
beginning and ending stone.
Do not abstract me, matter
screams, *I matter*. And the sound
is that long breath of radio
out of space, the sound of days'
frantic *amen*, which when night
comes catches in the mantle
making light sigh, and for moths
dying to become the light,
whom light shows, and who show light.
It is the pain of matter.

47

1

Koors Lucas+; Hans Lucas+; Jantje Jans+;
Josef Josefs+; Leendert Baalie+;
Jan Meir+; Gert Kok+; Piet Kok+; Wellem Kok+;

2

Hendrik Pieters+; Jan Plat+; Abraham Jaagers+;
Gert Schorpioen+; Kobus Stamper+;
 Minboor+; Klaas Naroo+; Piet Vanderwesthuise+;

3

Dooksteen Pokbaas+; Josef Josefs+.
Kok's people and Bergenaars, *weiboere.*
Memorialists, yes, their true marks.

48

1

(Neither here nor there, but I stopped
and stood to believe my eyes.
A country fell

2

into mountains like a war of angels.
Trivial, all. Beetles gossiped
in a reek of tar. I have said

3

there's nothing to it. Waste
bins overflowed and flies read what
was written there, and fat, and bones.)

49

1
Passing through: I, you –
all of you – the scarce viable
province, these pages.

2
It's as if we were practising,
in the round. But people
are brought out here, die here:

3
they are more real than black and white.
Suffer the Life, then, to kindle
your dust as tinder, to burn your book.

50

1
Lyddite+; Maxim+; Shrapnel+
plucking the sand within two
inches of me, a species of loneliness,

2
and once a charge of partridge shot,

                              no. 6,
cast its handful of gravel over my body.

3
This must have come of some shell,
no more
than a scatter of hail.

51

1

Forefathers that foresuffered my being bowed so
help me God, are they too cold, unblanketed?

2

I have become polyester. My skin dies
on me like a frost dust. I scratch the drove

3

lines into my shin. Wind plucks the dust
of me like a small smoke. I hear the thistle.

52

1

Out of the miscellaneous actions lost
at sea, this or that south-Atlantic barrage,
these ratings are turned on the great streams

2

to wash up on a sea-less sea, here confined
at Kalkfontein, Moddersee. What can they know
of the red westering flats, the scald,

3

questionable frost of such dryness?
Termitarial veterans of the *Graf Spee,* these
at table take a fork to their uncut hair.

53

1
What to do with the word
"concentration"?
Commissariat of spectacles, pencils.

2
Clerical war.
This is the estimate
of death. || of infants

3
dysentried, whole tents
shitting their skirts, skin sunk.
Human clay.

54

1

Arbousset, Casalis, Gosselin,
their Sinais, their first orthographies
brought down. Protestant rigours

2

so right in a high place, but French,
French? How does it frame its imaginary?
It must be said

3

English arrogates a realm
by treaty, blockhouse, railhead, barbed
wire. What you can do with wire.

55

1
Your unbeing being the saddest
part of me, the saddest country,
I stop for nothing.

2
Dread of what has already happened,
as hard as tar,
attaches all

3
the sudden detail to you.
You could not be
more near than the noon.

56

1
Windblown lark
dominant over gravel,
wire singing in the same air shoving
2
shrub and car,
shaking down the blue-
gum vapour
3
in a lazy affray.
The tree sloughs itself
down to the mint bone.

57

1

(The stranger took her up, covered
in a guise of clay and feathers.
She shook against him.

2

His horse was neutral. He turned to her
with a gall of paraffin and dust.
Weep into this strict putty he told her

3

and you will dream of whom brightly.
Whom will crawl with tears under the skin.
He watched her cross the fence and fly.)

58

1

Consider this high hubcap proffered
to a blue god. Its burnt
offerings pillar the proximate heaven.

2

Does sky care, that has flung
itself over love and war and called all
days? And is there a square

3

inch over which war was not
trotted out? It was your
concession into which pan blood was let.

59

1

Edenburg+ Modder River+ Jagersfontein+
What South African attempt
—at a town—has not

2

its race course? Saturday 25th of November
1899 and not a thought of the clod
diamonds. My battle array

3

                a blanket
and mackintosh, top boots, riding breeches, jacket of grey tweed.
Slouch hat.

60

1

Everything, everything, this falling
asleep. The beaten floor
of an aired shed, those just-necessary

2

acres, a tract of shrill thorns. Kept
heat, held chrism. The trove
catkins shine their scent to the bent air.

3

Farm your sleep and thorns, you
could gather there the tears of creation.
Pile the gold on buttered linen.

61

1
Send the blankets into the herd with sticks and dogs.
Look for the money, listen for the Scotch thistle and the rat.
There was sweet grass and there was sour and a drove

2
on the *trekpaaie*; keep up with time, keep up with me.
I will shave my skull, purge me, burn feathers,
honour the yard, burr the blankets. Time has got away

3
quick as khakibos in the droves. Everything here
worth one maybe one half more of a Caledon *muid*
if the tyres were sold before all perish, the rubber crumb.

62

1
Cronje only unafraid
(to use his constant
whip), white ostrich

2
feather in his hat. Goose
down from bed and pillows blow
free, half-buried feet

3
sticking out.
Burgherschap. I fail to see
where the "free" comes in.

63

1

No, nor Post-Truth, just outright lies, so
too soft-soap saying the said is soap.
There is breaking your life in two.

2

Words to bring it. I told you so.
Your sister died; words could not wash it.
Somewhere on the aortal N1 buoyed

3

for war. Occlusions of black absence
pock the sky like flak, some ominous prodrome
blackout. Panic. Grief. Or you.

64

1

Across the potatoes comes a breeze of television.
It stupefies the weekend. Blight blows in
from a neighbour's acre. In the scrapyard

2

of itself, a heron rots, feathers sodden. You
can call it politics, but there is no science of it.
Can you measure the bowels

3

wrung in a fist of lust, or take
the temperature of money? Can you assess the debt
looking back at the debtor in the mirror?

65

1

Conscionable respite, the sun in petrol
immolates at 8. The best seat in the house:
ankles in clay, where carp

2

gasp for a line, their ticket out. A body
of water sweats. Surely
these forms are not all cinema, the multitude

3

processing on the far shore? Stumbling
on vapour there they shuffle east to west,
whom night will hamstring, whom night will kneel.

66

1

Spare these. Spare even a thought
for these our *seed of peril*
in the state. Theirs is no

2

polity but goad and scourge, tools of the small
war brought by angels on the Land
of Nod. Indeed,

3

we are free to suffer and the thorough-
fare of days. Of no fixed address, drubbed out.
No rush. You can suffer tomorrow today.

67

1

Of the present and those not,
none is free. Of this rapid
muster of the dead, clueless
and akimbo, bones still pearl:
mouths somehow refuse the clay
like kissing. We own ourselves
by love unsafely made, or
is there any other way?
Even the dead are running
out of time, are come unstuck.
Nobody's out of the rain.

2

The graves are coming downhill,
sliding like shadow, cloudfall
down-slope, toppling ditch, rock, fence,
Saturdays and short months; now
their tenants will in no time
reach the road. To all a share
in this new common, sodden,
bought of the farm, now made
a middle of nowhere. Who
owns their share? Whose the borrowed
grader sunk in a puddling

3

clay? To each a part in that
field's weeping lesion. Shallow
ground down to the bone, this all
blank boneyard washed with drizzle
drifting over graves. A hand
drawn down its face and dropped.
This was unworked in one night
by a jackal weather. So
canvas rots and a blood seep
seethes in milk got free. Shroud
grass. And bells of buried frogs.

68

By some power of my hand I swear
on the stayed air or on the book that
my eyes have witnessed truly what
my hand has done.
Kebone

Deposition 1.
Morija, Basutoland. August, 1903.

By mine own hand

scraped into the plum
grit into the saffron
underdust these rusk
runes. ( )
                    Only that
(I——I) had talked with such saffron hope
that generations of shadow clapped one-handed
through the mountains waving the thunder:

(My eyes have seen what my hand has done)

( ) but the left hand ( ) (before) ( ) the egg of the stars ( )
we look from the last of us to the first (?days) ( )
( )
flanks of eland shamble in a gilt vlei:

flies, everything damsel, every beetle
aluminium, every fly butter, clambering
ground-mist, pygmy cranes, courting
the light, scintillate, iridescing, preposterous
as widows' trudgeon over grass, wings
incinerated, ashes and sparks, the words
the plough broke through, the plough

the eland drew

(plough of the sun
of the ridges, ridge-sun
plough of the world)

the world's share

(Here) ( ) were praises:

Loam-of-the-Air
Rising-Setting
Balloon-of-the-Khaki
Spore-of-the-Thorn
( )
First-of-Oxen
Hillside
Sand-the-Gun-Ploughed
Fist-of-Two-Fingers
The People
Cloud-of-the-Rain
Oxenfather
Crown(knuckle)-of-the-Moon
(I——I)
Here-You-Are

( ) in those (?)days.

69

1

These difficult tremendous poems
you writ on air
bee-furred with gold in that strut of light

2

fixed in a second-floor flat, edge of town
tending upon stalks and silks
bannering the maize belt, or

3

northern auriferous ground
upended in meal dunes, of sand
shucked, modified, attenuated, drear.

70

1

Sheep are baled against a farmhouse
wall for the shade. Ground heat: immemorial
stashed anthropogenic fire. 30 to Edenburg by baled

2

truck, further on foot. *Witgatspreeu* on staves
overscoring Doppler *continuo*, pipits
pull to the sun in their sideways ways. From there

3

might pry out sills and dykes, the military
sweep of irrigation armature and where turn-offs
go to.

71

1
Heat barges you like a fat boy, all bread.

Buzzard.

Now say what the world would. That your nose peeled
2
it was so white. That you ate cat. Pigeon.
Put a girl in danger in your circus,
forgot for her the cause of things becoming:
3
history, the men she fled, and you, that she
was your *inboekseling*. A bluegum tree.
There you strew cosmos over the blood ground.

72

1
There you made war.
There you took capital,
as Steyn did, for *this common enemy*,
2
and travelled troubled as Moshoeshoe
between redoubts, the mountain at night
and the plover's shoulder,
3
gathering in:
my lands being where my people are,
alienable and inalienable.

73

1

You want to know how it all ends? But no,
believe me you don't. Skies, earths,
it becomes them, nothing more.

2

Her strategy is owl, nearer the dead.
Days she lies up out of the story until
the story dies. Fire passes over her like your

3

eyes and she flies up an owl on fire. In the burnt
tent of herself she coughs a winter. She's gone;
her fugitive eyes are reading this.

74

1

Rain. And the company rain keeps
cowers in thrilled pity of itself to see
the Good vouchsafed delight of getting wet.

2

Crossing a paragraph of the first rain,
even at itself surprised at having come to this,
because what is accomplished is at last,

3

see: sky shows capillaries at the back of its eye,
unseals its dreams in abashed clouds
of mustard and champagne, and weeps.

No god so terrible
as a sky god for us
cathedralled in our eye's
dome. No agate, hemmed lith
or hard iron cuts it. So
we supplicate, so grasp,
discovering with hands
held out to the first rain
our want of the earth. Steeped
in the water that comes
between sky and stone, we
accrue not as trove but as
time's precipitate, as
sinter of the earth.

uHlanga

POETRY FOR THE PEOPLE

— ALSO AVAILABLE —

Foundling's Island by P.R. Anderson

White Blight by Athena Farrokhzad, translated by Jennifer Hayashida
IN ASSOCIATION WITH ARGOS BOOKS, USA

Zikr by Saaleha Idrees Bamjee

Milk Fever by Megan Ross

Liminal by Douglas Reid Skinner

Collective Amnesia by Koleka Putuma
CITY PRESS BOOK OF THE YEAR 2017

Thungachi by Francine Simon

Modern Rasputin by Rosa Lyster

Prunings by Helen Moffett
CO-WINNER OF THE 2017 SOUTH AFRICAN
LITERARY AWARD FOR POETRY

Questions for the Sea by Stephen Symons
HONOURABLE MENTION FOR THE
2017 GLENNA LUSCHEI PRIZE FOR AFRICAN POETRY

Failing Maths and My Other Crimes by Thabo Jijana
WINNER OF THE 2016 INGRID JONKER PRIZE FOR POETRY

Matric Rage by Genna Gardini
COMMENDED FOR THE 2016 INGRID JONKER PRIZE FOR POETRY

the myth of this is that we're all in this together by Nick Mulgrew

AVAILABLE FROM GOOD BOOKSTORES IN SOUTH AFRICA & NAMIBIA
& FROM THE AFRICAN BOOKS COLLECTIVE ELSEWHERE

UHLANGAPRESS.CO.ZA

Printed in the United States
By Bookmasters